THE CLASSICAL COLLECTION FOR GUITAR TAB

Arranged by Alexander Glüklikh

MW00574021

EDITOR: Aaron Stang
COVER DESIGN: Robert Ramsay

Copyright © 1992 CPP/Belwin, Inc.
15800 N.W. 48th Avenue, Miami, Fl. 33014

Special thanks to my wife COLEEN for all of her support, inspiration and encouragement.

This book is dedicated to the memory of my son ARTHUR.

CONTENTS

INTRODUCTION

This song collection was created to add more variety to the guitarists repertoire. Some of the pieces in this collection have never before been available as guitar arrangements. The music has been written in standard notation and tablature to make it accessible to all guitarists regardless of their background. Performance notes have been included in order to facilitate a better understanding of both the musical and technical demands of each piece.

A. Glu

Romanza

Performance Notes:

Romanza is one of the most popular songs ever written for the guitar. The song is in 3/4 with a flowing triplet accompaniment. The quarter note melody falls mainly on the first string and is also the first note of the eighth note triplet accompaniment figure.

This arrangement consists of two parts – the traditional arrangement and a variation in tremolo style. The two sections can be played separately or together.

If you are unfamiliar with the tremolo technique, I recommend taking Ex. 1, which consists of a diminished chord moved chromatically up and down the neck, and practicing it until you achieve a smooth flowing tremolo. The tremolo should sound like one uninterrupted line – similar to a mandolin style melody with a simple arpeggio accompaniment (played by the thumb).

I also recommend taking the same exercise and practicing it with a different combination of right hand fingers (p m a m). This will help you to increase the flexibility of the "weak" ring finger (a).

Ex. 1 (Also try with p m a m).

ROMANZA

ANONYMOUS
(19 Century)
Arranged by ALEXANDER GLÜKLIKH

Romanza – 5 – 1

8

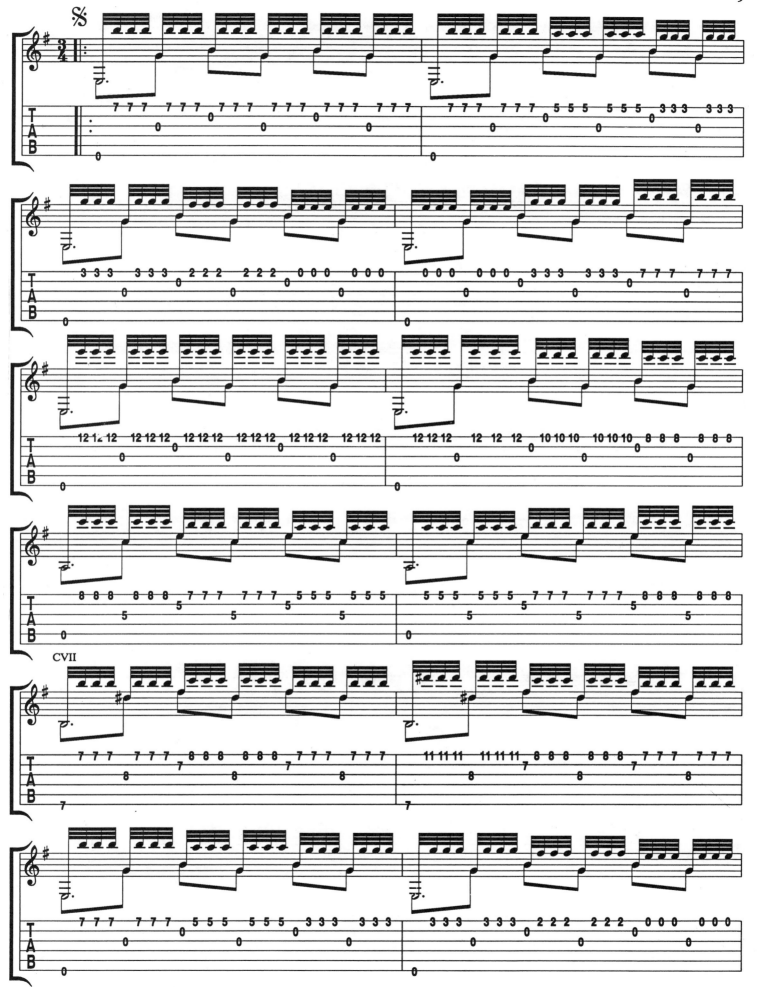

10

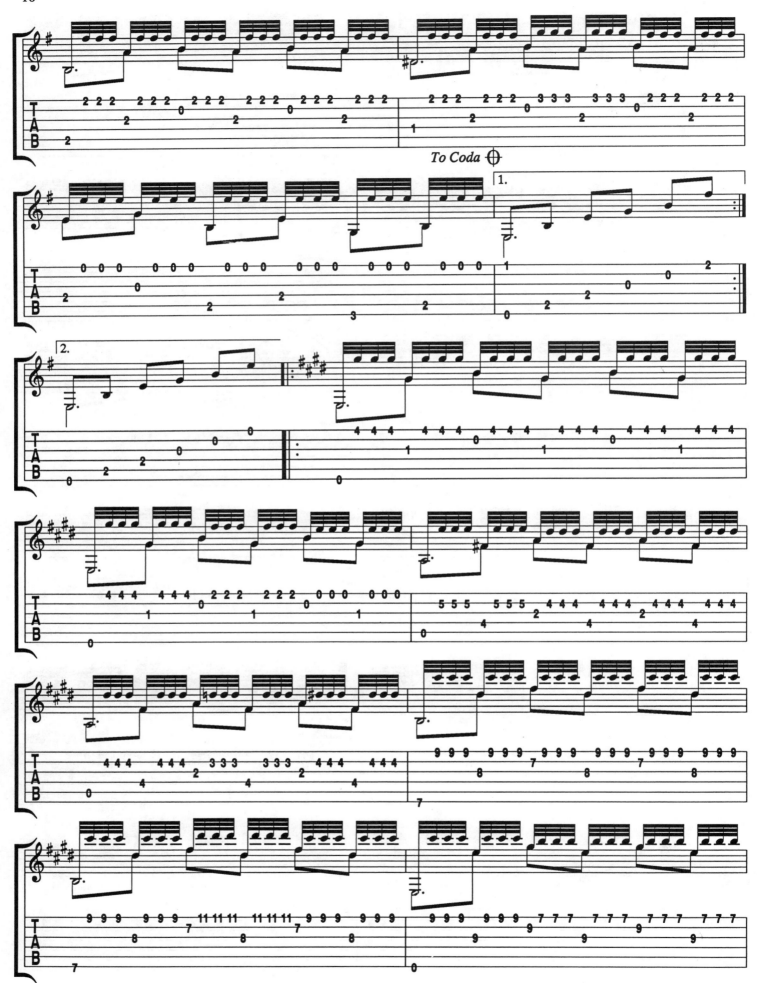

To Coda ⊕

Romanza – 5 – 4

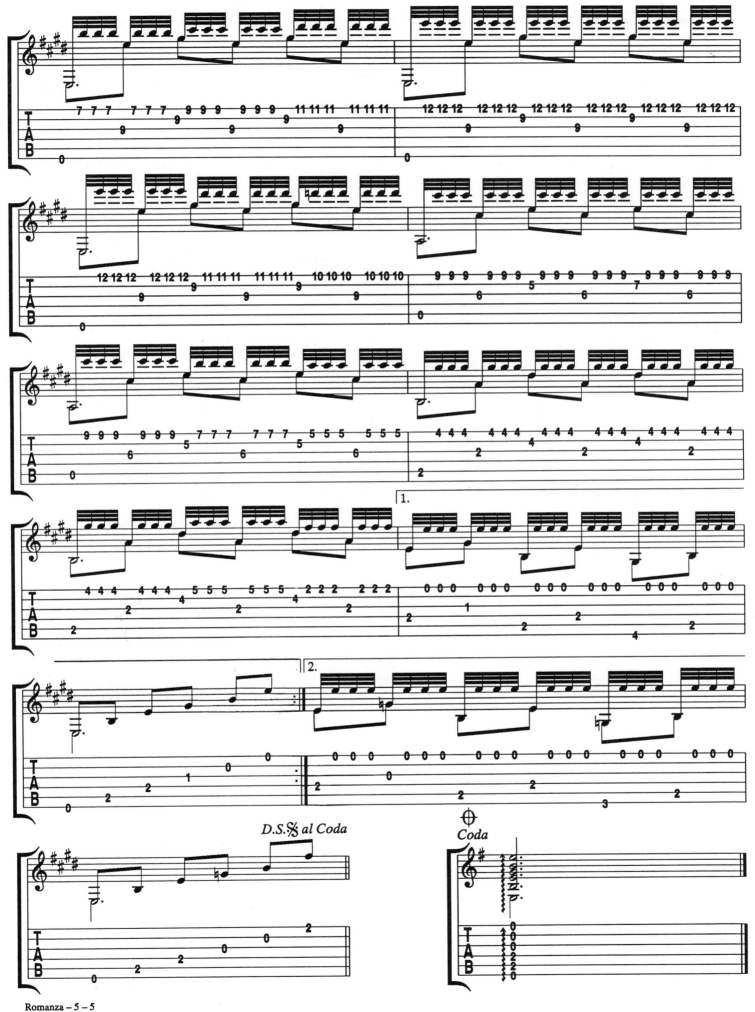

Romanza – 5 – 5

Prelude No. 1/Ave Maria

Performance Notes:

Charles Gounod used J. S. Bach's Prelude No. 1 as the harmonic basis for the very beautiful and popular Bach/Gounod Ave Maria (not to be confused with the Schubert Ave Maria). Prelude No. 1 is the first prelude in Bach's "Well Tempered Clavier", a collection of forty-eight preludes and fugues written for keyboard. In this arrangement both pieces can be performed separately or together.

I have written out the chord progressions to both pieces in order to facilitate a direct comparison of the two works. Notice that the chord progression to the Prelude No. 1 is very similar to what we would expect to find in most modern popular music.

Beginning in bar 20 of Prelude No. 1, Bach heightens the tension of the piece and delays the final resolution to the tonic chord by first moving away from the tonal center (C), and then using a G pedal tone in the bass (bars 25 – 32). Then, just when you expect a resolution to C, instead he moves to C7, followed by an F/C and G7/C before finally resolving to the tonic C.

Harmonic Analysis, Prelude No. 1:

C	Dm/C	G7/B	C	Am/C	D7/C	G/B	C	
Am	D7/F♯	G	Gdim7	Dm/F	Fdim7	C/E	F/E	
Dm7	G7	C	C7	Fmaj7	F♯dim7	Fm6/A♭	G7	
C/G	G7sus	G7	Cdim7/G	C/G	G7sus	G7	C7	
F/C	G7/C	C	‖					

Harmonic Analysis, Ave Maria:

C	Dm/C	G7/B	C	Am/C	D7/C	G	C	
Am	D7	G	Gdim7	Dm/F	Fdim7	C/E	F/E	
Dm7	G7	C	C7	Fmaj7	F♯dim7	Cm/G	Fm6/A♭	
G7	C/G	G7	./.	Cdim/G	C	G7	./.	
C7	F/C	G7/C	C	‖				

PRELUDE No. 1

J. S. BACH

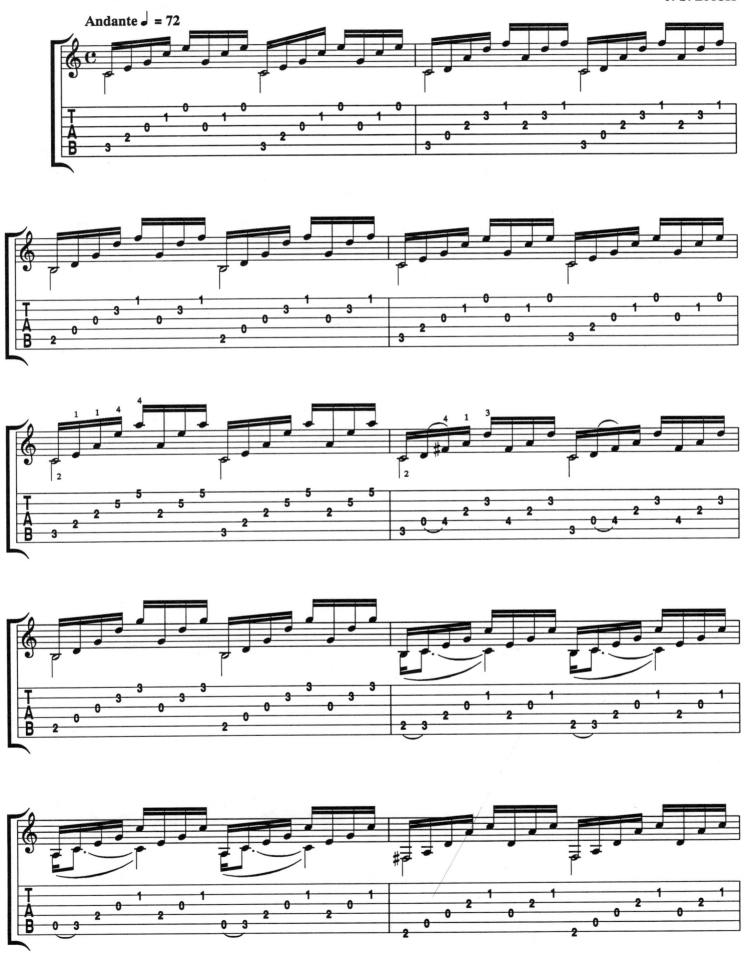

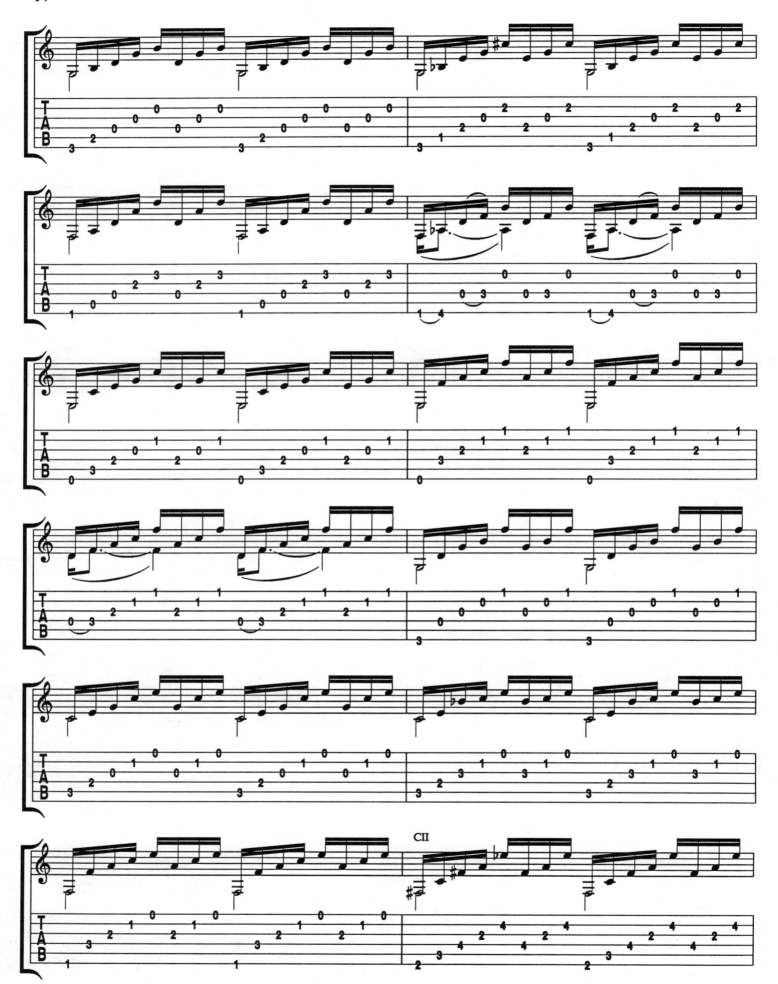

AVE MARIA

Ave Maria by BACH/GOUNOD
Arranged by ALEXANDER GLÜKLIKH

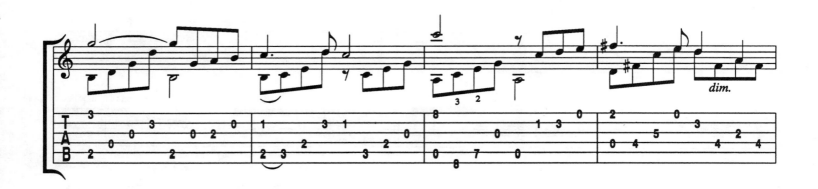

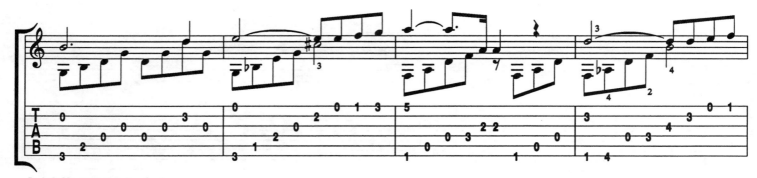

18

The Four Seasons

Performance Notes:

Antonio Vivaldi (1678 – 1741) wrote a number of "programmatic" concertos – works that tell a story, or carry some meaning outside the music. The most famous of these concertos is The Four Seasons, which Vivaldi published in 1724 as Op. 24: "The Contest Between Harmony and Invention". Each of the four movements represent a specific phenomena associated with each season – birdsong in the spring, summer thunderstorms, fall harvest, and shivering in the winter. Along with the concerto, Vivaldi published a set of sonnets outlining the events they portray.

The four movements of this arrangement for solo guitar, presented here as a suite of themes from "The Four Seasons" may be played separately or together. The original order is: Spring, Summer, Autumn, and Winter. (The music is presented here in the order: Summer, Spring, Autumn, and Winter to prevent cumbersome page turns.)

Spring
This is one of Vivaldi's most recognized melodies. The accompaniment consists of broken octaves, played by the thumb. (Those of you familiar with the "Travis picking" style will find this very familiar.) The theme should be bright and lively. A clear distinction between forte and piano should be made to create an echo-like effect.

Summer
Tune your 6th string down to D. This piece should be played rather slowly and very legato. Despite the frequent rests it is important that the melody move forward smoothly.

Autumn
This song should be played brightly with a march-like feel.

Winter
There is a continuous flow of the 16th notes between the melody and the accompaniment. Much of the piece requires the use of a barre finger. Carefully note the barre positions and fingerings in order to achieve a smooth, flowing performance.

THE FOUR SEASONS
(A Suite of Themes)
Theme From "SUMMER" Op. 8, No.2
Movt. 1

ANTONIO VIVALDI
Arranged by ALEXANDER GLÜKLIKH

Theme From "SPRING" Op. 8, No. 1
Movt. 1

ANTONIO VIVALDI
Arranged by ALEXANDER GLÜKLIKH

The Four Seasons – 7 – 3

Theme From "AUTUMN" Op. 8, No. 3
Movt. 1

ANTONIO VIVALDI
Arranged by ALEXANDER GLÜKLIKH

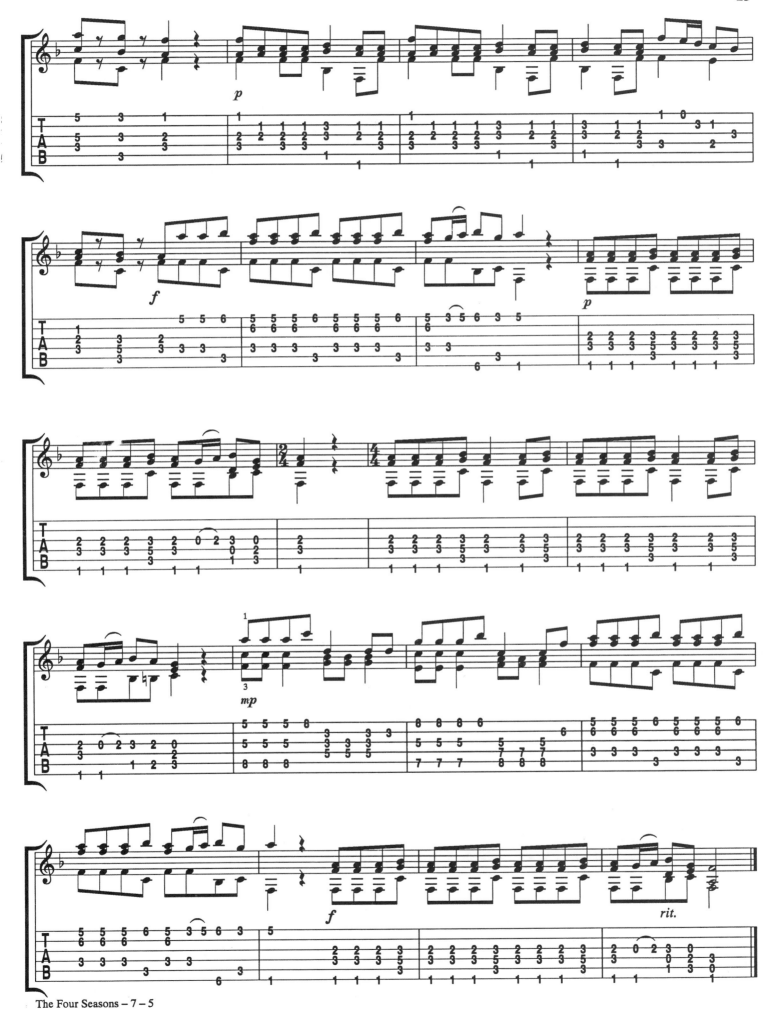

The Four Seasons – 7 – 5

Theme From "WINTER" Op. 8, No. 4
Movt. II

ANTONIO VIVALDI
Arranged by ALEXANDER GLÜKLIKH

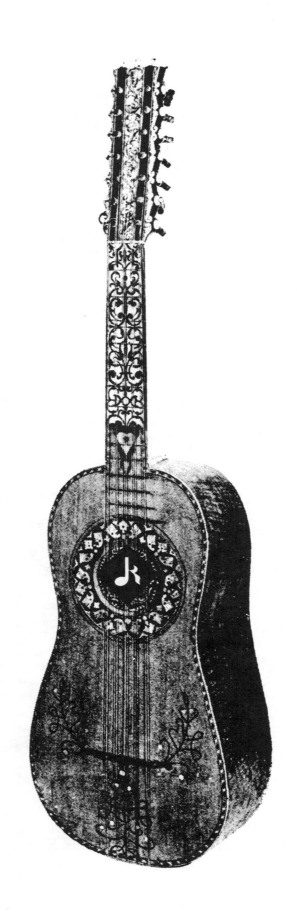

Greensleeves

Performance Notes:

Greensleeves is one of the most popular and enduring melodies ever written. This old English folk song was mentioned twice by Shakespeare in the "Merry Wives of Windsor", and by other writers of this and later periods. During the British Civil War of the 17th century, Greensleeves was used by the Cavaliers as a setting for many political ballads. The song is equally well known as "What Child Is This?", the popular Christmas song.

In this arrangement, the melody is played primarily in the bass, on the 4th string, with a simple arpeggio accompaniment played above it. With the exception of the open G string in measure 5, the melody should be played by the thumb.

The stem directions separate the melody from the accompaniment. The melody is down stemmed and the accompaniment is up. I recommend that you practice playing the melody only, before playing the complete arrangement.

GREENSLEEVES

ANONYMOUS
(16th Century)
Arranged by ALEXANDER GLÜKLIKH

Gently flowing ♩ = 120

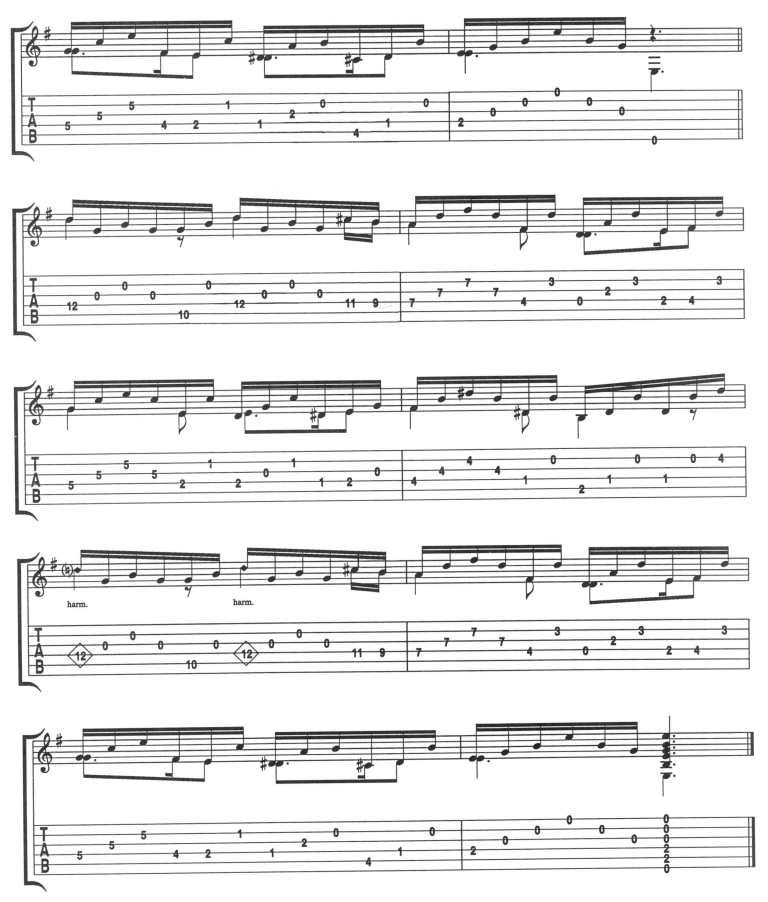

Greensleeves – 2 – 2

Moonlight Sonata

Performance Notes:

It was with the genius of Ludwig van Beethoven that the Classical Era reached its climax. Beethoven, whose figure overshadows the whole of 19th century music, was born in Bonn, Germany in 1770, the son of a court musician.

Beethoven wrote masterpieces in each of the musical genres practiced during his time, among them are the 32 sonatas for piano. One of his most famous sonatas is No. 14, the "Moonlight Sonata." This piece works remarkably well on the guitar and utilizes the full range of the instrument.

Eighth note triplets are used throughout. The "Moonlight Sonata" should be played slowly and with great expression. Special attention should be paid to measures 25, 26, 35, 36, 48, and 49 in order to maintain smoothness. Measures 32 through 37, which consist mainly of diminished arpeggios, are marked with a crescendo; be careful to maintain a constant tempo. In the last 10 measures the melody shifts to the bass.

MOONLIGHT SONATA

LUDWIG VAN BEETHOVEN
Arranged by ALEXANDER GLÜKLIKH

Adagio sostenuto ♩ = 53

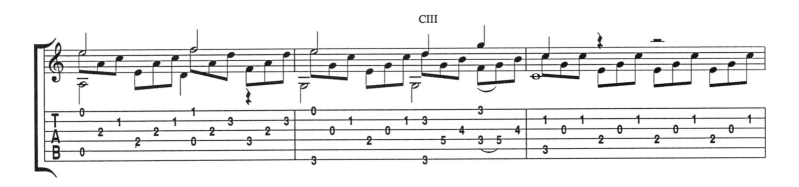

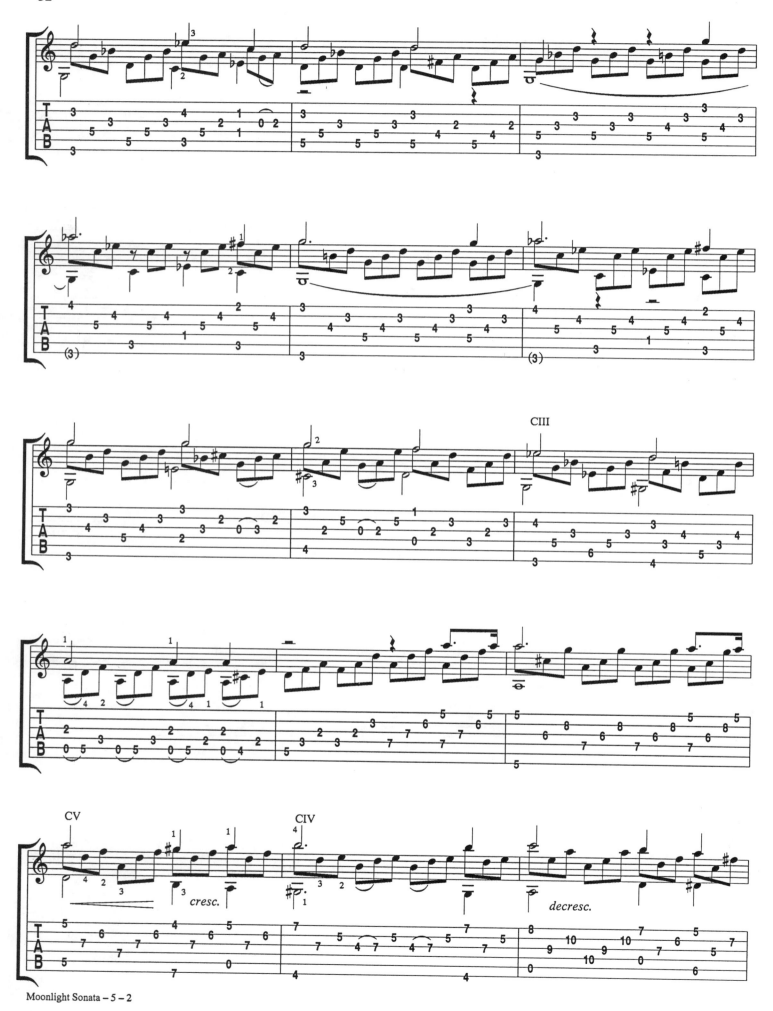

33

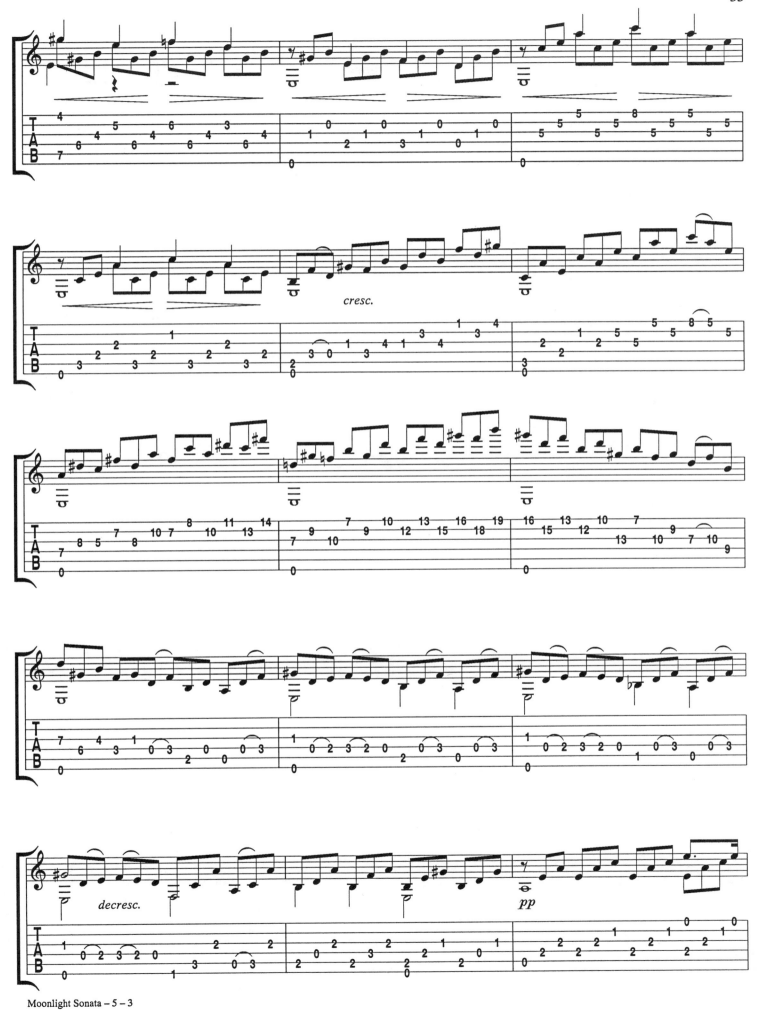

Moonlight Sonata – 5 – 3

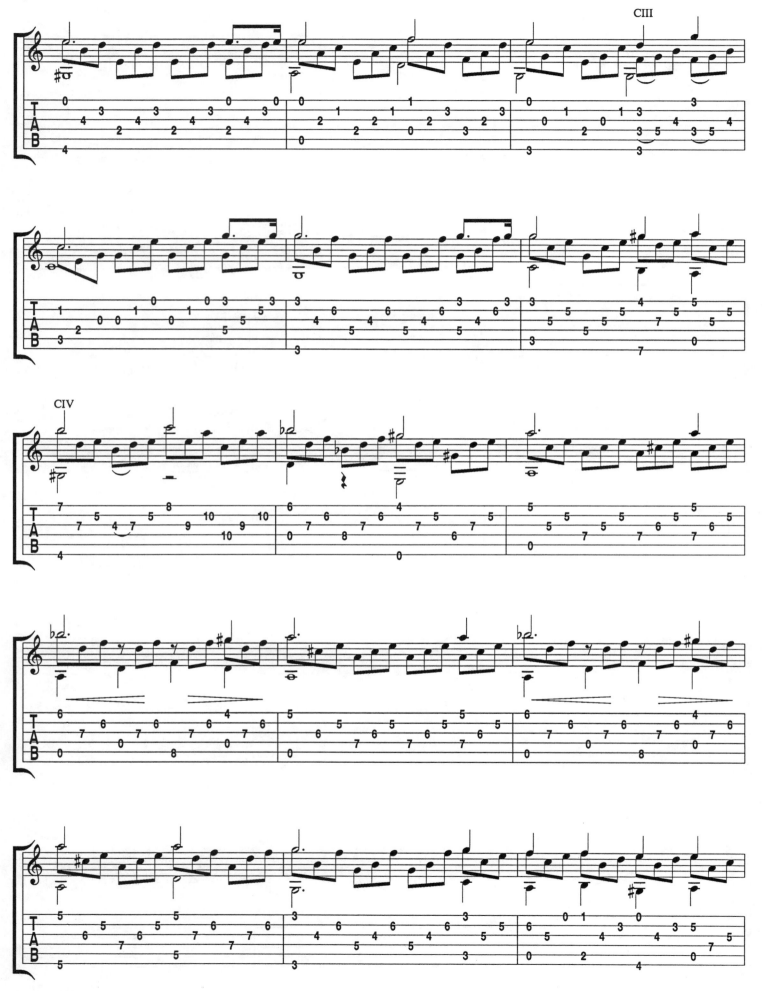

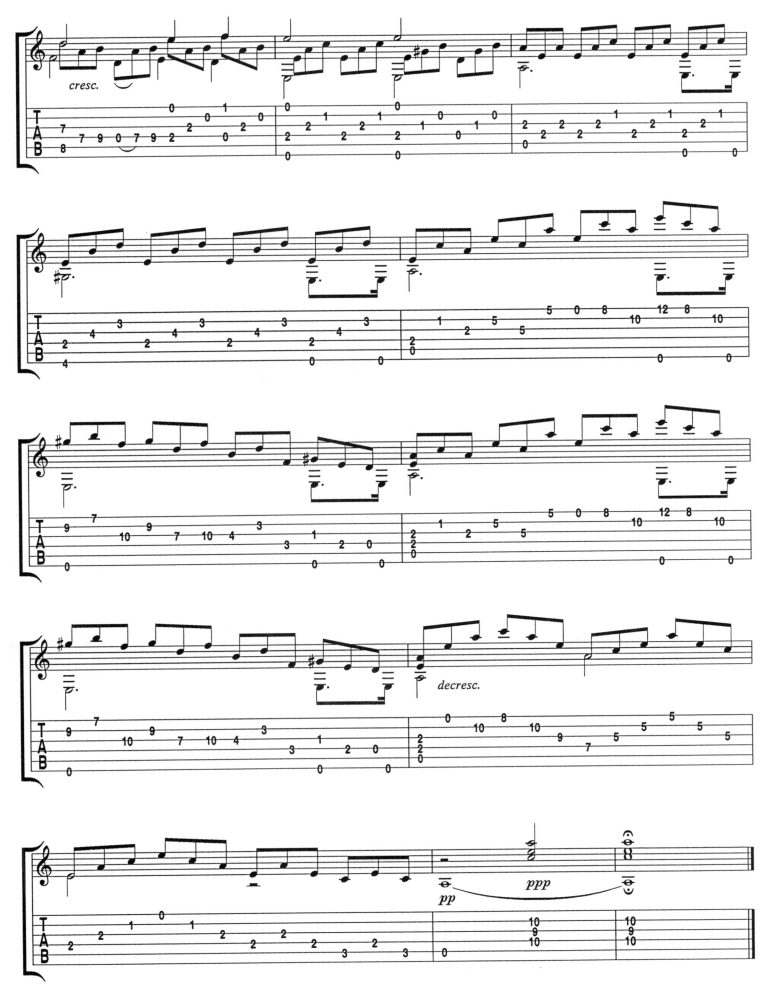

Moonlight Sonata – 5 – 5

The Swan

Performance Notes:

This piece has been transposed from the original key of G to D to make it playable on the guitar. The low E string must be tuned down to D. In order to enhance this beautiful melody, the tremolo technique has been applied to this arrangement. It is important that all notes of the tremolo are played evenly.

If you are unfamiliar with the tremolo technique, I recommend taking Ex. #1, which consists of a diminished chord moved chromatically up and down the neck, and practicing it until you achieve a smooth, flowing tremolo. The tremolo should sound like one uninterrupted line--similar to a mandolin-- with a simple guitar accompaniment (played by the thumb). In order to strengthen your fingers and gain complete control of this technique, I recommend that you practice this exercise, alternately accenting each part of the beat, first accenting all notes played by the thumb (p), then the index finger (i), the middle (m), and the ring finger (a).

You should also practice the melody separately (not in tremolo). This will help your interpretation, and make it easier for you to separate the accompaniment from the melody. Ex. #2 shows the first four bars of the melody, when not played with a tremolo.

THE SWAN

CAMILLE SAINT-SAËNS
Arranged by ALEXANDER GLUKLIKH

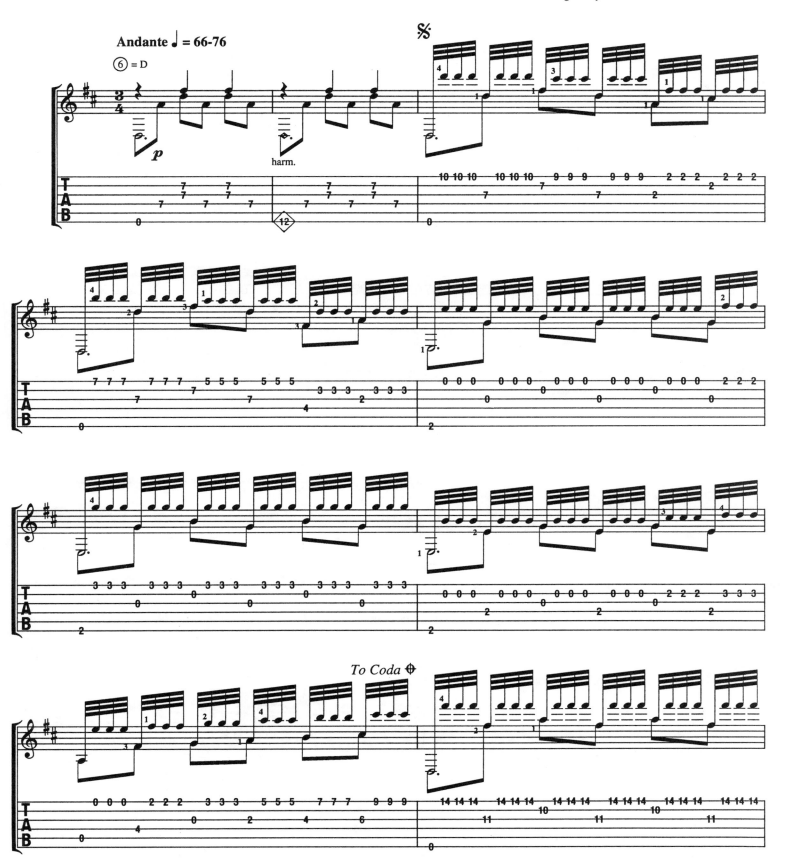

38

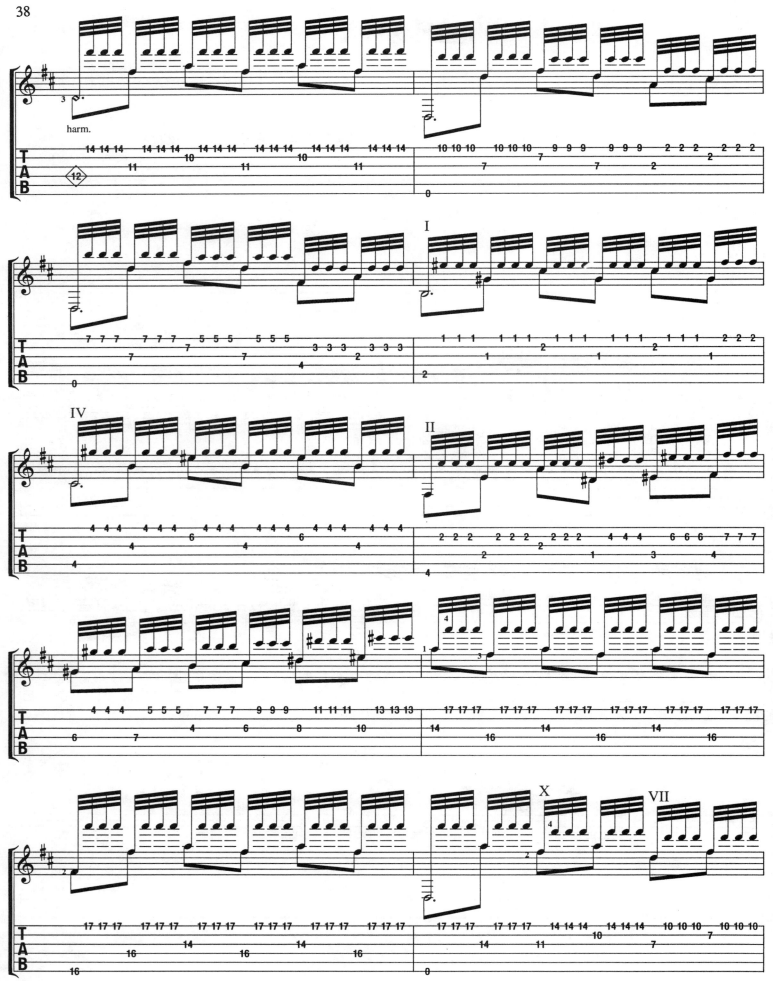

The Swan - 5 - 2

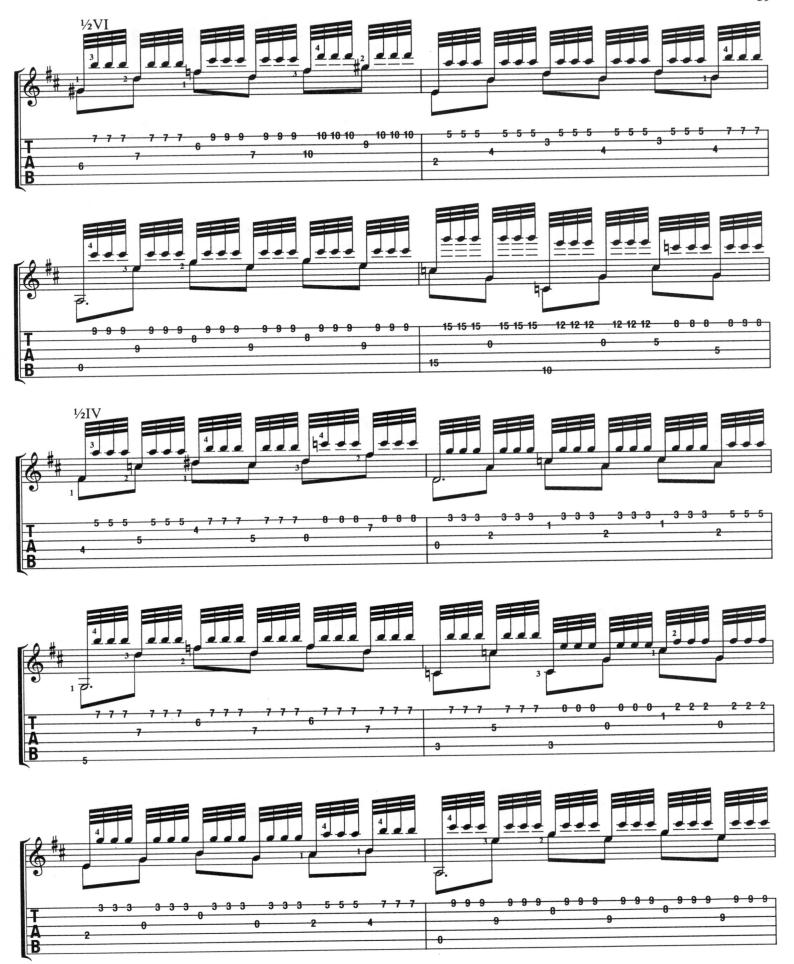

The Swan - 5 - 3

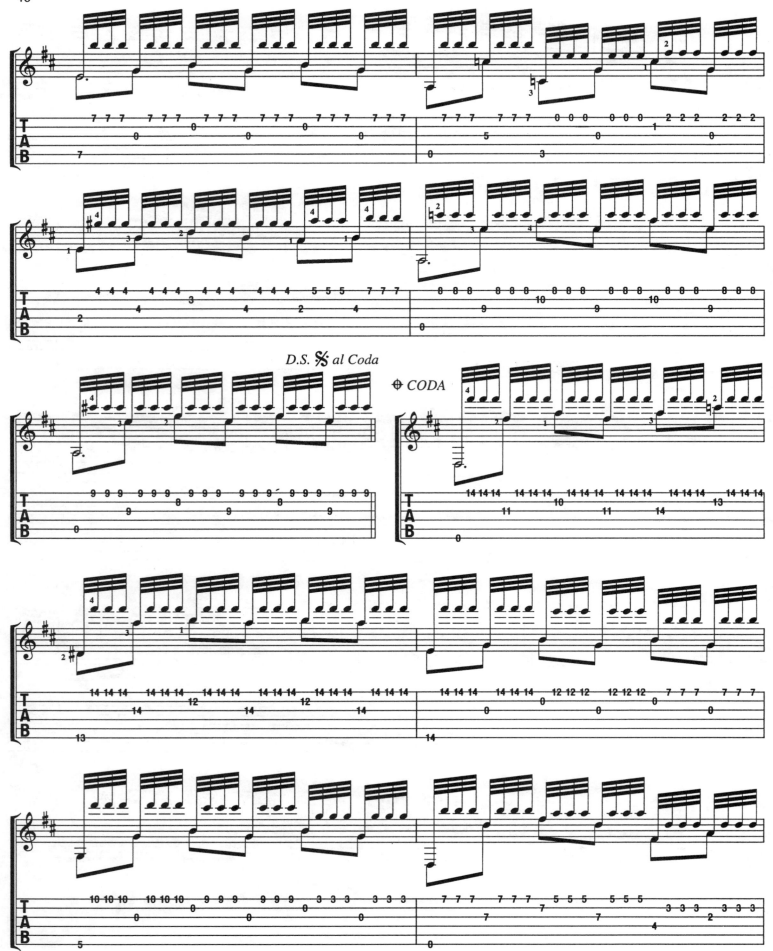

D.S. 𝄋 al Coda

⊕ CODA

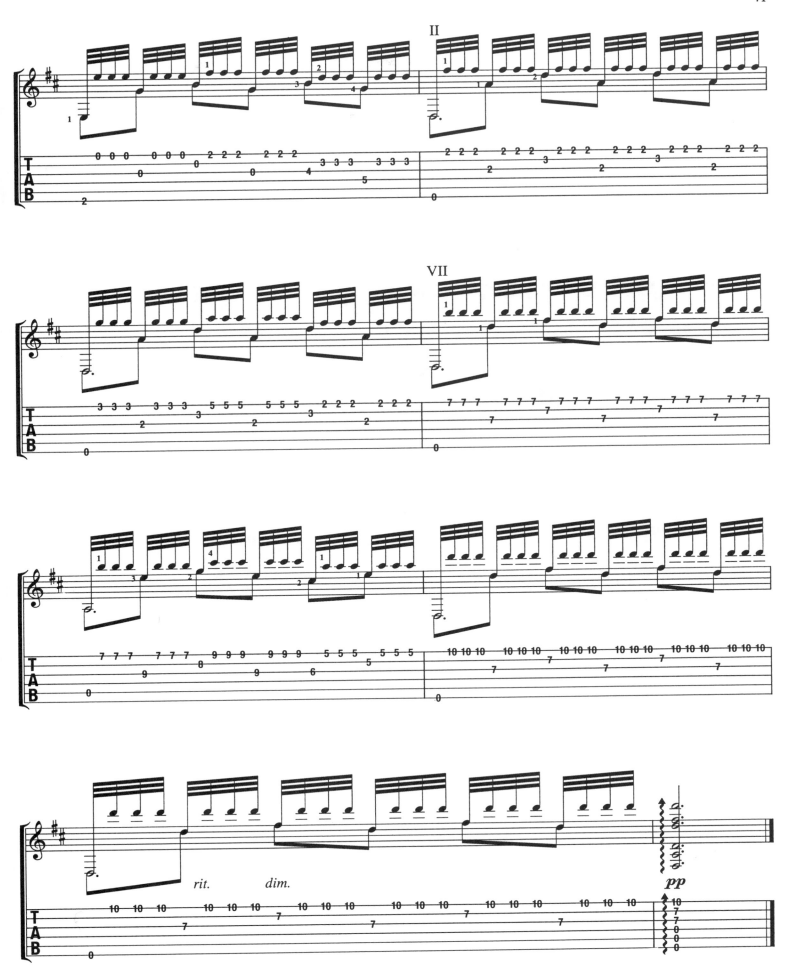

Dark Eyes
Variations on a Theme

Performance Notes:

Dark Eyes is one of the most popular and recognizable of all Russian folk songs. This arrangement consists of the main theme and three variations.

The theme is comprised of the melody (written with stems up) and a simple arpeggio style accompaniment in 16th notes.

The four note arpeggios in the theme are replaced by groups of six in the 1st Variation. Throughout the theme and 1st Variation the melody is played on the 4th string.

The 2nd and 3rd Variations consist of jazz-like linear improvisations on the melody.

The tempo should remain constant throughout the piece, with the exception of the cadenza, which should be played freely.

DARK EYES
(Variations on a Theme)

RUSSIAN FOLK SONG
Arranged by ALEXANDER GLÜKLIKH

Moderato (♩ = 112 - 120)

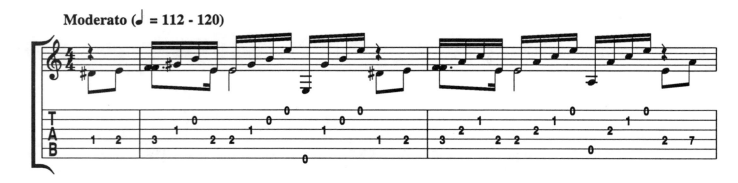

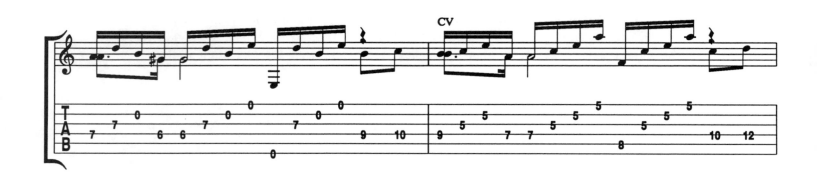

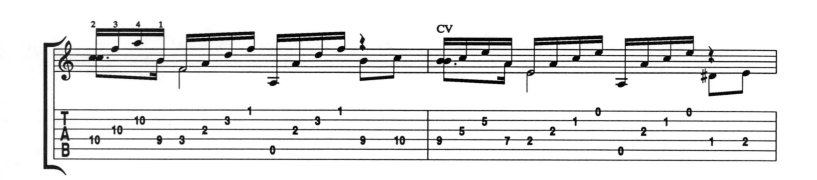

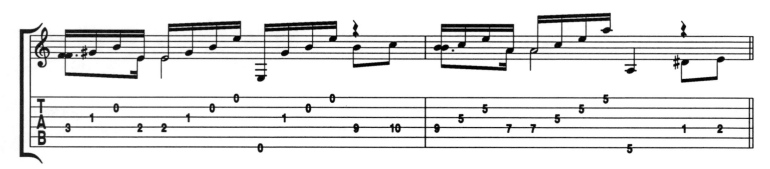

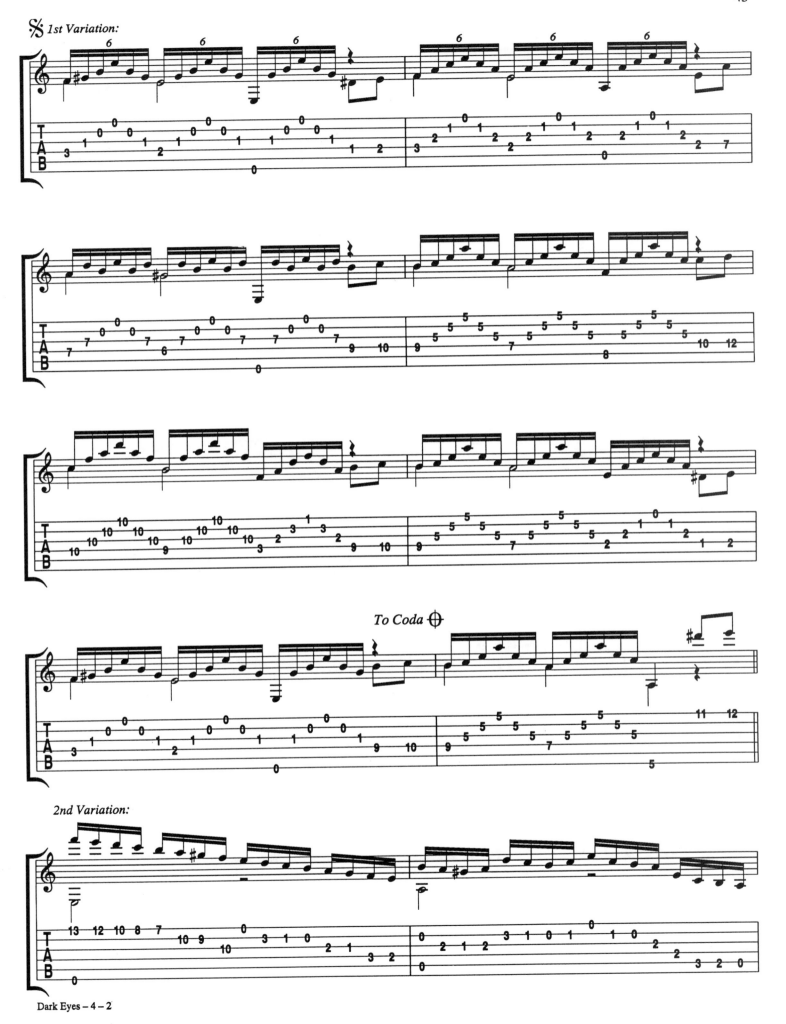

Dark Eyes – 4 – 2

3rd Variation:

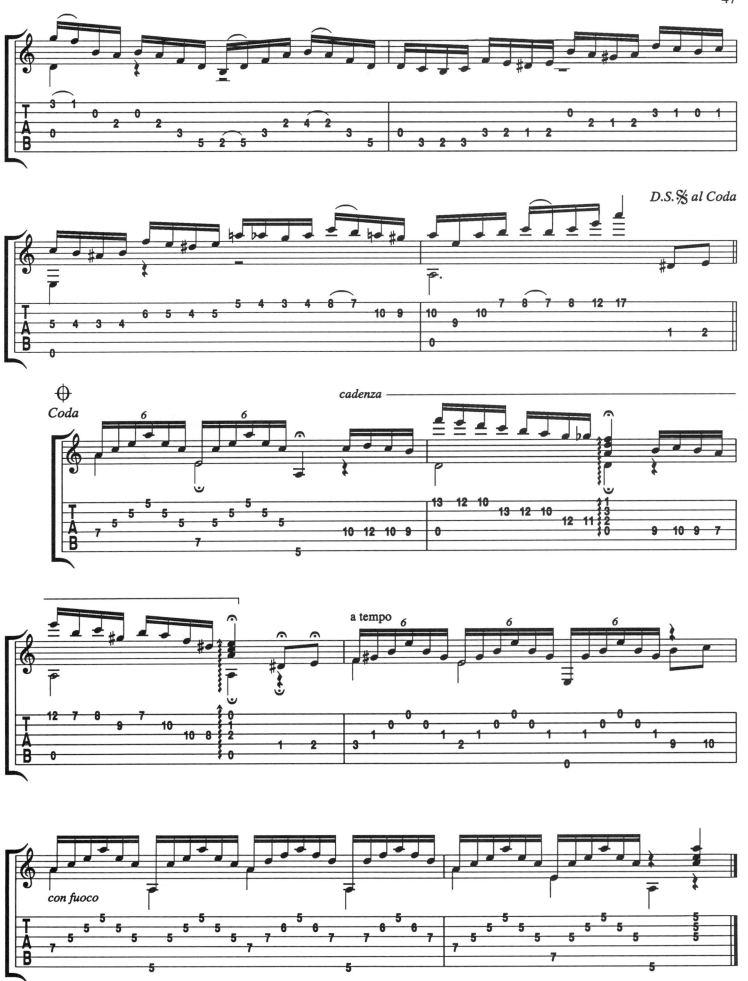

ABOUT THE AUTHOR

A native of Riga, Latvia (part of the former Russian Empire), Alexander Glüklikh was born in 1949. He began studying the guitar at the age of 12, and after music school in Riga, Alex was drafted into the Russian army where he played guitar, French horn and balalaika in the military band. After the service Alex performed throughout the Soviet Union as a solo guitarist. He has also toured with some of Russia's finest musicians as a member of the Oleg Lundstrem Orchestra, based in Moscow.

Currently, Alex Resides in Miami where he teaches and performs as both a classical and jazz guitarist.